DORSET
The Glorious County

ROGER HOLMAN

HALSGROVE

First published in Great Britain in 2007

Copyright words and pictures © Roger Holman

Images on pages 97-100 reproduced by courtesy of the Lulworth Estate

Title page photograph: Poole Harbour.

British Library Cataloguing-in-Publication Data
A CIP record for this title is available from the British Library

ISBN 978 1 84114 586 0

HALSGROVE
Halsgrove House
Ryelands Farm Estate, Rockwell Green
Wellington, Somerset TA21 9PZ
email: sales@halsgrove.com
website: www.halsgrove.com

Printed and bound by Grafiche Flaminia, Italy

INTRODUCTION

When in 1991, Roger Guttridge, Roger Lane and I collaborated to produce our first book *The Landscapes of Dorset*, little did I think that six books and fifteen years on I would still be photographing and writing about the Dorset landscape. It was then, and still is, a labour of love. But as a landscape photographer what else could it be. I can trace my Dorset ancestry back eight generations and maybe they were here a long time before that, so I think I am entitled to be a little prejudiced about the beauty of Dorset.

So what is it that attracts so many people to holiday here and then sometimes to settle? It is a county without a motorway and not many dual carriageways either. It has no cities and no towns of any size. The cost of housing is high but it is ironic to think that in 1900, when there was just one building at Sandbanks, you could have bought a plot for a few pounds and now it is claimed to have one of the most expensive land costs in the country if not the world.

Well for sure the coast is a big draw, part of which has now been awarded the accolade of World Heritage status with the likes of the Grand Canyon and the Great Barrier Reef. The Dorset section starts at Ballard Down near Old Harry Rocks and runs all the way down to Lyme Regis; it then continues into Devon until it arrives at Exmouth. This designation should preserve and protect it for future generations. For the residents, it is a double edged sword, more fame, more people, but we shouldn't deny the countryside to others and look on it as our own personal preserve. Lulworth for instance becomes very busy in summer; but even then, once you strike out along the coast path, people seem to magically vanish.

It is in its infinite variety that the coast excels; possessing the huge natural harbour of Poole, safe sandy beaches, towering chalk cliffs and the rugged coastline with its coves and bays. Many counties can boast these attributes but none I think all within just a 70-mile length of coast. However, nowhere in the world possesses another Chesil Beach. You need only to stand at the top of Portland to appreciate the immensity of this 9-mile-long stretch of pebbles getting gradually smaller until they turn into fine shingle at Burton Bradstock. Roger Guttridge writing in *Landscapes of Dorset* has the best description of it. 'The Chesil Beach is not so much a piece of coastline, more a natural wonder of the world. For millions of years it has greedily reaped a harvest from the tidal ebb and flow, always adding to its store of pebbles, giving few away. They come in many forms, from the rocks of many places, some of them far distant. If it were possible to weigh them, they would tip the scales at fifty million tons; if it were possible to load them into lorries, the convoy would stretch from England to Australia.'

Portland is another of Dorset's famous landmarks. It is a bare, almost treeless landscape scarred by centuries of stone quarrying, standing 500ft above the sea. Hardy named it the 'Gibraltar of Wessex' and although called an island, it isn't, being tethered to the mainland by Chesil Beach. John Leland noted in 1540 'The people be good in the flinging of stones and use it for the defence of their isle.' They also made good use of the oolite rock as a very desirable building material with at least six million tons of Portland Stone used for the rebuilding of London after the great fire. Inigo Jones used it for the rebuilding of the Whitehall Banqueting Hall, and Christopher Wren, for St Paul's Cathedral. The area of Weymouth and Portland will again be in the public eye when the 2012 Sailing Olympics are held there.

But it doesn't end there. Unlike some counties which have a good coast and not very interesting hinterland or visa versa, we have both. There are the heath lands that Hardy immortalised in his books and the chalk hills that start near Shaftsbury and roll south and west down to the sea at Lyme. This creates the great vales of Blackmoor and Marshwood with many stunning vistas from the summit of the hills. It is also the reason there are many Iron Age hill forts. Hutchings lists twenty five, of which Maiden Castle and Lamberts Castle are but two. Of course later on the Romans came to civilise us and there remains much to remind us of their occupation. Who can stand on Ackling Dyke and not visualise Vespasian's legions tramping that same road two thousand years ago?

Running through the Stour and the Frome valleys are the two Dorset rivers and their tributaries, which with their numerous water mills, provided food and work for generations. Although there are

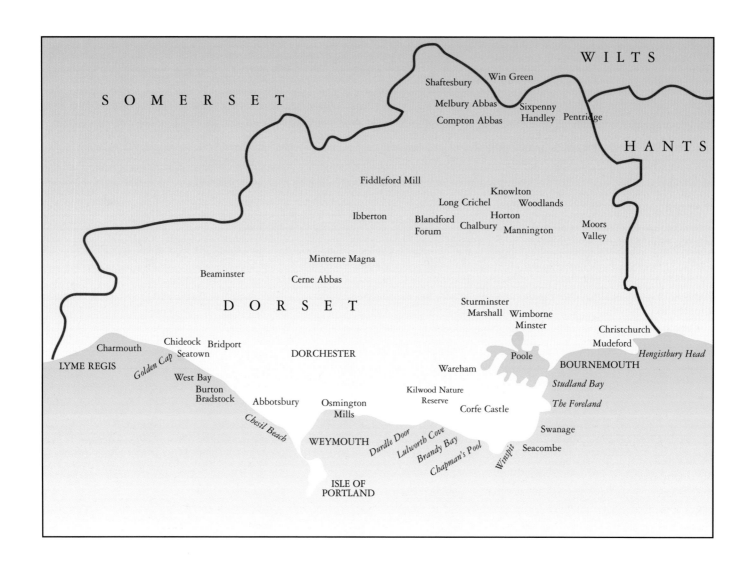

WILTS

SOMERSET

Shaftesbury
Win Green

Melbury Abbas
Sixpenny
Handley
Compton Abbas
Pentridge

HANTS

Fiddleford Mill

Knowlton
Long Crichel
Woodlands

Ibberton
Blandford
Forum
Horton
Chalbury
Mannington
Moors
Valley

Minterne Magna

Beaminster
Cerne Abbas

D O R S E T

Sturminster
Marshall
Wimborne
Minster

Christchurch
Mudeford
Charmouth
Chideock
Bridport
Seatown
DORCHESTER
Poole
BOURNEMOUTH
Hengistbury Head
LYME REGIS
Golden Cap
Wareham
Studland Bay
West Bay
Burton
Bradstock
Kilwood Nature
Reserve
The Foreland
Abbotsbury
Osmington
Mills
Corfe Castle
Chesil Beach
Durdle Door
Lulworth Cove
Swanage
WEYMOUTH
Brandy Bay
Chapman's Pool
Winspit
Seacombe

ISLE OF
PORTLAND

no longer any full time working mills, the rivers themselves winding through lush meadows with contentedly grazing cattle, provide us with an attractive and timeless landscape.

How much change has there been and what of the future? Dorset was, and still is, mainly an agricultural county. It is fortunate that roughly 80% of the population resides in about 10% of the county in and around the eastern conurbations. There is an average annual new build rate of 1800 homes in the whole of the county and it is estimated that by 2028 there will be a 15% increase in population, which doesn't seem too great for that time span. The development that has taken place, appears to have been absorbed without too much effect and the further one travels west, the more one feels that very little has changed over the years. Most farmers farm with nature conservation in mind. Field margins are left untouched to help preserve wildlife, and a certain amount of acreage is also designated 'set aside', while hedges are no longer being ripped out. During the foot and mouth problems the landscape was denuded of cattle but they have shown a revival and there seems to be more sheep farming.

Projected wind farms in Dorset have so far failed to get planning permission but it is felt that smaller installations may be more successful, especially as it has been decreed that within ten years all new houses will need to be carbon neutral. Farmers will probably be growing new crops such as elephant grass to produce bio fuels.

The Dorset Wildlife Trust's 'Rebuilding Dorset's Biodiversity' is a major initiative for the Trust and its partners. The concept is to restore large 'landscape' areas of the county, linking fragmented habitats to land rich in wildlife, alongside flourishing and sustainable communities.

One aspect of the landscape that I have always found particularly jarring is the line of high voltage pylons and cables that straddle the county. It is unrealistic to hope that this can ever change, for to bury them is a highly expensive and complex undertaking. But there has been a relatively small amount of money allocated to remove some of the lower voltage pylons. Any reduction is to be commended.

Of course there has been a lot of social change. A great deal of the working population would have toiled on the land but now the service industries absorb a good proportion of the work force. What has become particularly noticeable is the vast increase in road traffic over the last few years. Between 1991 and 2001 there was an increase of 28%. The existing car parks are quite often full to capacity. During the winter season there used never to be any difficulty in finding a parking space but now that is not the case. One certainly gets the impression from the planners that we are unlikely to see dramatic changes in the foreseeable future. That is probably what most Dorset inhabitants would wish but how the projected increase in car ownership can be managed without major road building is a problem that will have to be solved.

I am often asked which camera and film I use and whether or not I have gone over to digital. Yes, I do use a Nikon D2x digital camera but have certain reservations about digital capture for landscape work. It is certainly very convenient, and about 10% of the pictures in this book are taken with it, but my preference is still for film. There is an indefinable quality about film that I find difficult to describe.

Regarding film I, like most landscape photographers, prefer to use Fuji Velvia, but Fuji have recently stopped producing it, claiming that they were unable to obtain the necessary raw materials. The replacement film was not particularly well received, so we all bought up what stock was still available and made room in our fridges. However, there are rumours that it may come back next year.

As far as the cameras are concerned, all are medium format. Mamiya RZ, Pentax 645N and a 5x4 Cambo Wide. It is easy to feel that the camera is the most important part of the process but in reality it is not. I am always reminded of a little story that a good friend of mine relates when he is talking to groups about photography.

This photographer produced a marvellous picture which was enthused over by someone he knew. 'What a beautiful picture' she said, 'you must have a very expensive camera.' A little later the photographer was invited to one of her dinner parties. When they had finished, he complimented his hostess and said 'That was a tremendous meal, you must have a very expensive cooker.'

Landscape photography requires a lot of time, a lot of patience to repeatedly go back to the same place until the light is deemed the best it's going to get, and last but not least, a very tolerant wife. Fortunately I possess all three, and I might add, Rosemary is very supportive and a great proof reader!   **Roger Holman**

Previous page: Weymouth.

Above: Hengistbury Head. On a clear day, the Isle of Wight appears as if it is a continuation of the mainland.
Once iron ore was mined here but it is now a nature reserve guarding the western side of Christchurch Harbour.

Right: From the top of Hengistbury Head can be viewed this valuable
piece of real estate in the form of a double row of chalets.

Above: The Isle of Wight from Mudeford.

Left: Mudeford. Situated on the eastern side of Christchurch
Harbour and guarding the narrow entrance.

Above: Christchurch Harbour and Priory from Hengistbury Head. Both the Hampshire Avon and the Dorset Stour end their journeys in Christchurch Harbour. Being quite shallow it cannot accommodate boats of any size but due to the shallows and reeds it has become an ideal habitat for a vast number of birds. I would question the wisdom of allowing a modern development to be built so close to the Priory.

Right: Christchurch Priory across the Stour just before the river enters the harbour.

Christchurch. The River Avon
in early morning as it drifts
lazily through the town.

The weir at Eyebridge.
This is where the Roman
soldiers would have crossed
the Stour on the road between
Hamworthy and Salisbury.

Boscombe Pier. Just before sunrise the sky turns orange and silhouettes the pier.

Bournemouth Pier with Sandbanks and the Purbecks in the distance.

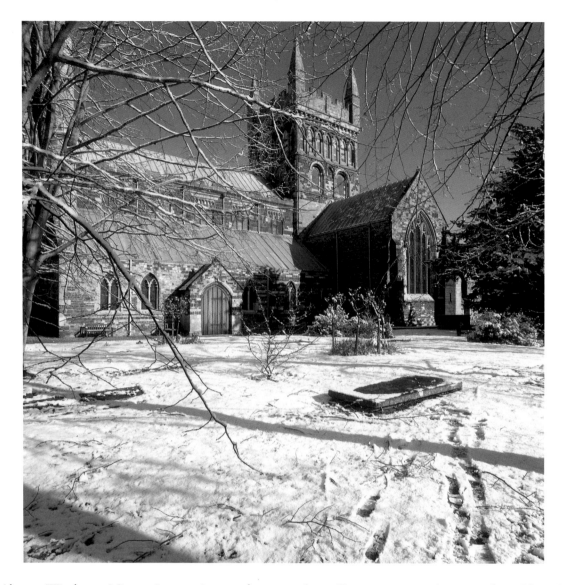

Above: Wimborne Minster is an ancient market town that still manages to retain some of its old world character. It is dominated by the Minster that has looked down on the life of the town for centuries.

Right: The River Stour flows through the water meadows that surround the town. Fortunately much less flooding occurs now than in days gone by.

The Stour at Canford Bridge.

Flooding at Canford Bridge.

Right: Swans on the
Stour at Cowgrove.

20

Above: Chalbury Church.
A delightful little church, parts
of which date back to the thirteenth
century. The west end was rebuilt
in the eighteenth century.

Left: Stour water meadows on
a frosty morning before the
sun has burnt off the frost.

Beech Avenue, Badbury Rings. The famous avenue of pollarded beech trees, planted by French prisoners after the Napoleonic Wars, is regrettably gradually disappearing due to age but still looks impressive.

Above: Badbury Rings. The National Trust, which owns the land,
grazes sheep to help keep the turf in good condition.

Right: Moors Valley Country Park, owned and run by the East Dorset
District Council, has proved a tremendous success as a family attraction.

Above: Mannington Heath.

Right: Gussage All Saints at harvest time.

Horton Tower. Jo Draper in her Dorset guide book says 'It looks like a disused factory' but I think it is quite majestic standing on the top of a hill surrounded by green pastures. There is surprisingly little history recorded about it but by general consent it seems that it was built for Humphrey Sturt in the eighteenth century as an observatory for him to watch the hunt when he became too old to participate or, as I was once told 'to keep an eye on his young wife'. It makes a nice story anyway!

Below: Winter and the old man. This old man used to collect wood regularly from the nearby forest for his fire accompanied by his faithful dog. It was taken during one hard winter before Vodafone took over the tower for renovation prior to mounting their aerials.

Horton. Every year a few acres of longer stem corn is grown and threshed in the old traditional way to provide thatch, although a great deal is now imported, mostly from Turkey.

Above: Winter morning at Cowgrove near Wimborne.

Right: Cranborne Chase opens out before you, viewed from Chalbury Hill. The Horton Inn strategically located on the crossroads has served travellers for hundreds of years. It is difficult to visualise how the Chase must have looked in the thirteenth century when it was a huge forest and King John hunted here.

The grounds of St James's Church Alderholt, burst forth in
springtime with a wonderful display of wild daffodils.

Whitemill Bridge, Sturminster Marshall. One of the oldest and most attractive bridges in Dorset photographed on a lazy summer day. I had to wait a long time for the two horses to separate, which they did briefly before turning and going back up the bank.

Winter at Whitemill. The mill, now owned by the National Trust,
has been renovated and is open to the public.

Harvest time at Long Crichel.

Gussage All Saints Church.

Left: Bowerswain near
Gussage All Saints. There is
something very appealing
about the sun breaking through
early morning mist.

Above: Knowlton. This was once the church of a now deserted medieval village. It is unusual in as much as it is built on the site of a Neolithic henge monument. Some people find it a little eerie, perhaps because of the human sacrifices that were once supposed to have been made here.

Right: Knowlton silhouetted against a most unusual cloud formation fashioned like a trumpet.

Above: Fontmell Down. Owned by the National Trust and the
Dorset Wildlife Trust, it provides great walks with magnificent views.

Left: A glade near woodlands in the snow.

Above: Melbury Hill from Compton Down.
These two pictures show how dramatically the same location alters with the seasons.

Right: Looking toward Pentridge from near Cranborne.

Above: Win Green, a well known landmark is just visible on the horizon. Although inside the
Wiltshire boundary the photograph is taken from Dorset so I feel entitled to include it in the book.

Left: Near Sixpenny Handley. Some people object to the huge rape fields
that have become a part of the landscape but I love the vibrancy of the yellow rape flower
against the blue sky, although it is at its best for only a very short while.

Above: Melbury Abbas from Melbury Hill. The quintessential English
village with church snuggled down in the valley.

Right: Compton Down from Melbury Hill.

Ashmoor is the highest
village in Dorset and is surrounded
by woods which are carpeted by
bluebells in springtime.

Melbury Hill and the grand sweep of country from the top of Zig Zag Hill.

Above: Shaftesbury, Gold Hill. Made famous by a Hovis advertisment – it manages to retain the same nostalgic atmosphere.

Right: Child Okeford from Hambledon Hill. The views from this Iron Age hill fort are spectacular, particularly north and west overlooking the Blackmoor Vale. The little known Clubmen made their last stand here where they did battle against Cromwell's troops. It was not so much that they opposed Cromwell but they resented the depredations of the soldiers on both sides.

50

Above: Many photographers succumb to what I call 'The lone tree syndrome' and can't
resist photographing them. This is one at the base of Hambledon Hill.

Right: Fiddleford Mill. No longer a working mill but otherwise little seems to have changed over the centuries.
It stands next to one of the earliest manor houses in Dorset and is looked after by the English Heritage Trust.

Dorset Steam Fair. A huge annual gathering of steam engines, claimed to be the largest in Europe, with people and engines arriving from all over the world.

Blandford Forum's annual Georgian Street Fair. The Corn Exchange is reflected
in the trumpet of the musician of the Band of the Royal Corps of Signals.

The River Frome as it leaves Dorchester and wends its way on towards Wareham and Poole Harbour.

Bluebells and rape in the Purbecks.

Above: Poole Harbour.

Left: Brownsea from Evening Hill. It was inevitable that Poole, blessed by its huge natural harbour would become an important port for commerce. It is also an ideal recreational area for sailors and wind surfers.

Poole Harbour. Dawn breaking over Poole Quay.

Poole Harbour. This is the area reserved for the working boats. Some fish are still landed here.

Poole Harbour. Waiting for the tide to come in. Obviously the two men thought it worth dragging their boat towards the water's edge to gain a few minutes of extra sailing.

Above: Compton Acres. The breathtaking Japanese garden is just one of a number of themed gardens at Compton Acres that are open to the public.

Left: Evening near the Haven Yacht Club.

Studland Bay. Owned by the National Trust, it is arguably one of the best beaches on the South Coast with safe bathing backed by extensive sand dunes. This was taken early one winter's morning after strong winds the previous night. All traces of footprints have disappeared leaving ripples in the sand.

Studland Bay. Frost on sand. Taken early one frosty morning, it is unusual to see frost on the beach but on this particular morning there had been a hard frost and the low sun had thawed one side of the sand dune.

The National Trust has designated an area as a naturists' beach so when I came across this, it struck me as being quite amusing. Someone with a sense of humour.

65

Above: Swanage. Some people feel this architecture is not in keeping with the town but I find it quite attractive.

Left: Sunrise. Old Harry Rocks from Studland Bay.

67

Left: Swanage. Rough weather in winter.

Travelling west, Handfast Point makes a very dramatic start to the Jurassic Coast.

Corfe Castle. It is such an iconic image that it warrants at least two pictures. Bequeathed to the National Trust by Ralph Bankes as part of the Kingston Lacy estate it stands on a steep-sided hill guarding the only gap in the line of the Purbeck Hills. Ironically it seems to me to be much more impressive in ruins than had Cromwell's men not got to work on it. The buildings seem to grow out of the hill rather than having been built upon it. Some years ago I visited Osaka in Japan and was staggered to walk into the hotel lobby and be confronted by a huge 20-foot mural of Corfe Castle.

Arne. The RSPB nature reserve also has a large deer population. Early in the morning the deer seem to be quite unfazed by seeing people strolling through the woods to the eastern shore of Poole Harbour.

Seacombe. One of the cliff-edge quarries.

Above: Winspit. Another cliff-edge quarry. Just imagine the danger of loading
huge blocks of stone into waiting barges in anything other than a flat calm sea.

Right: Purbeck hills seem to fold one into another so you are not
sure of where one starts and one finishes.

Above: Kilwood Nature Reserve owned by the Dorset Wildlife Trust. It is the site of nineteenth-century clay workings. The scent of wild garlic hangs heavily in the air here and in many other parts of the Purbecks.

Right: Storm clouds hanging over the Coastguard Cottages at St Alban's Head.

Above: Chapman's Pool and beyond spread out before the summit of Emmetts Cliff.

Right: This is the last wild and isolated stretch of coast left in Dorset, due to much erosion of Emmetts Cliff and the steep access. A lobster fisherman is probably the only person you are likely to meet here.

Overleaf: Chapman's Pool.

Above: Wareham Quay. It is difficult to believe that in medieval times Wareham was the major port rather than Poole, but when the Wareham channel silted up it ceased to be of importance.

Left: From Sywre Head looking west.

Above: Wareham. Early morning on the River Frome.

Right: Wareham Church on a frosty morning with a pink sunrise.

The River Frome at Ridge just before it flows into the harbour.

Right: Storm Clouds brewing over the sea, silhouetting the Clavel Tower.

Kimmeridge Bay. When tide and wind are favourable, the Kimmeridge Ledges make it an ideal location for wind surfing. It is overlooked by the Clavel Tower. At the turn of the last century it was possible to safely drive a coach and four between the tower and the cliff edge but due to erosion it has become dangerously close to toppling over the cliff. Fortunately enough money has been raised to dismantle and rebuild it some 25 metres further back and then it will come under the jurisdiction of the Landmark Trust and be used as a holiday let.

The small waterfall that tumbles over the cliff top into Kimmeridge Bay is one of the few in Dorset.

Sunset over Kimmeridge Bay.

Right: Brandy Bay, Hobarrow Bay and Gad Cliff from Kimmeridge.

90

Gad Cliff. Pick a clear day when the army ranges are open and walk from above Kimmeridge to Worbarrow Bay. For a walk that is not too strenuous by Purbeck standards, you will be rewarded with the most superb views.

Worbarrow Bay. A ten minute walk is required from the car park at Tyneham.

Above: Mupe Rocks. Looking eastward at low tide.

Left: Mupe Bay. Situated between Worbarrow and Lulworth, it is isolated and
seldom visited although the coastal footpath runs above it.

Moon rising over
Arish Mell from Mupe Bay.

St Oswald's Bay looking towards Durdle Door.

Previous pages: Lulworth Cove. A romantic cove that was formed when the small stream breached
the hard limestone barrier and allowed the sea to enter and wash out the inner softer clays behind
It is the jewel in the crown of the Jurassic Coast.

Above: Cerne Abbas is surrounded by hills and remains famous or infamous because of its giant.
However, it has a lot more than that to offer. Even the curse of the car doesn't seem to destroy the old
world charm, which I'm sure is a joy to its inhabitants. Some American friends of mine own a property there
They spend any available time they can at Cerne and consider it one short step from heaven.

Left: Sun setting over the coast from Lulworth Cove.

The Blackmoor Vale. Thomas Hardy called it 'The Vale of the Little Dairies'.

Ibberton is tucked under Bulbarrow Hill, that looks down on
an archetypal English village cricket scene.

Ibberton. A farmer walks his geese back home.

Minterne Magna. Looking down from Little Minterne Hill to the seat of the Digby family.

Previous pages: Egerton Hill. An Iron Age hill fort that provides stunning views over the surrounding countryside and sea. It is claimed that the famous smuggler Issac Gulliver planted some pine teres on the summit to act as a seamark for his smuggling ships, but they were eventually felled on the orders of the Revenue men.

Looking east from the massive cliff of White Nothe. Between Bats Head and Ringstead the shoreline is inaccessible but that is amply compensated for by the stunning views as you walk the cliff path.

Cows grazing on the headland overlooking Ringstead Bay.

Above: Osmington Mills sunset at low tide.

Left: Portland from Osmington Mills.

Above: Weymouth Harbour at eventide.

Left: Weymouth Harbour. Very popular with the sailing fraternity but also a
busy working port where a good deal of fish is landed and from where the fast
Condor Catamaran service runs daily to the Channel Islands and France.

Left: Portland Lighthouse warns shipping of the dangerous rocks and the Portland Race.

Portland. The Pulpit Rock.

Portland.
A carving of a stone
mason overlooks
Chesil Beach.

Right: The view from
above Abbotsbury of
The Fleet, Chesil and
Portland before the sun
has risen above the
horizon.

116

Above: The Fleet. An 8-mile-long lagoon enclosed by Chesil Beach.

Right: The Chesil Beach. Considered by some to be another wonder of the world, it is quite unique, stretching some 9 miles. It is claimed that smugglers and fisherman coming ashore in fog could identify where they had landed by the size of the pebbles for they are graded along its whole length, being smaller at the western end. The shingle shelves off very steeply and has been the graveyard of many a ship. Hardy called it Deadman's Bay and indeed swimmers need to treat it with the greatest of respect.

118

St Catherine's Chapel stands alone on a hill overlooking Abbotsbury and The Fleet. Built in the fourteenth century, it has long been a seamark for sailors, which is probably why it survived the Dissolution of the Monasteries. It is certainly worth a climb to the top for the views as well as to visit the chapel, but one marvels at the dedication of the worshippers who were obliged to do it regularly of necessity. Perhaps not so much for the spinsters who could pray in the chapel for a husband on one day a year.

Left: A solitary swan makes its way across The Fleet.

Pages overleaf: St Catherine's Chapel overlooking the Chesil Beach. This prominent rainbow only lasted a few minutes but for once I was lucky enough to be in the right place at the right time.

Pilsdon Pen is an Iron Age
hill fort and standing at 908 ft is
the highest hill in Dorset.

Lewesdon Hill is just a few feet lower
than its sister hill Pilsdon Pen from
where this was photographed.

Lamberts Castle is another Iron Age hill fort
overlooking the Marshwood Vale.

Above: Beaminster pronounced 'Bemminster' was a place of some importance on the road between Yeovil and Bridport but these days seems a delightful backwater beneath the road from Toller Whelme.
In Edwardian days Sir Frederick Treves had nothing but good to say about it, which was praise indeed.

Left: Looking west from Lamberts Castle above the Marshwood Vale.

127

Burton Bradstock marks the western end of the Chesil Beach beyond which
the coastline changes dramatically. The cliff faces are subject to much erosion,
some being weathered into strange shapes like protruding rows of bared teeth.

Burton Bradstock. It is amazing how soon the sea greedily absorbs all the cliff falls, leaving little trace, bar a much reduced distance between the cliff edge and the coastal path.

Burton Bradstock looking east.

The magnificent face of East Cliff, West Bay with the cliffs of
Burton Bradstock in the background.

131

The new pier has now been completed at West Bay replacing the old one that
made the entrance to the harbour a hazardous experience in rough weather.

The harbour at West Bay.

Colmer's Hill. A very prominent landmark that most people seem to remember. That is probably because it is a small but regular steep sided hill topped by a few pine trees and seen against the sky on the A35 just beyond Bridport. The Dorset Craft Guild used it as a basis for their logo.

Looking back to Bridport from Quarry Hill early one autumn morning.

Above: Seatown and Golden Cap in winter.

Right: Seatown and Golden Cap from East Ebb.

Left and above: Chideock hugs the lower slopes of Golden Cap. It is the last remaining community
of any size on the A30 that does not have the benefit of a by-pass, having to rely on
a road built for horse and coach to support twenty-first century traffic.

Above: Golden Cap with a covering of snow taken from near Cain's Folly.

Left: Golden Cap. The view from the summit shows the extent of
the erosion that has occurred in the area of The Spittles.

Above: Charmouth Beach and Golden Cap

Right: Charmouth. The Cob at Lyme Regis is just visible below the setting sun.

Evening at Lyme Regis.